D...

b...

us all.
Some really lovely
quotes in this book
just for you.
Love you always
unconditionaly
mum a dad
xxx

Published in 2012 by Helen Exley Giftbooks.
Design, selection and arrangement © Helen Exley Creative
Ltd. 2012.
Copyright © Helen Exley Creative Ltd. 2012.
**Illustrations by Angela Kerr © Helen Exley
Creative Ltd. 2012.**
The moral right of the author has been asserted.

12 11 10 9 8 7 6 5 4 3 2 1

ISBN 978-1-84634-595-1

**Helen Exley Giftbooks, 16 Chalk Hill,
Watford, Herts WD19 4BG, UK.**

www.helenexleygiftbooks.com

Be True
to Yourself

Illustrations by Angela Kerr

A HELEN EXLEY GIFTBOOK

ABOUT THIS BOOK

The quotations in *Be true to yourself*
talk about bringing integrity,
kindness, fairness and courage
into our work, our families
and our daily lives.
The book encourages us to follow
what we believe in, to take risks,
and to live our personal values
to the full. As Janis Joplin,
the folk singer put it,
"Don't compromise yourself.
You're all you've got."
It is a powerful little book!

Be the change you want to see in the world.

MAHATMA GANDHI
(1869-1948)

Principles are eternal....

WILLIAM JENNINGS BRYAN
(1860-1925)

*A*ll that there is
to the making
of a successful, happy,
and beautiful life,
is the knowledge and
application of a few
simple, root principles....

JAMES ALLEN

It's doing small things
for the love of each
other – just a smile,
or carrying a bucket
of water, or showing
some simple kindness....
It's not how much
we give, but how much
love we put in
the doing....

MOTHER TERESA (1910-1997)

You are
What you are
by what
you believe.

OPRAH WINFREY,
B.1954

*O*ur great and glorious
masterpiece is to live
appropriately.
All other things, to rule,
to lay up treasure,
to build, are at most
but little appendices
and props...

MICHEL DE MONTAIGNE
(1533-1592)

The real things haven't changed. It is still best to be honest and truthful; to make the most of what we have; to be happy with simple pleasures; and have courage when things go wrong.

LAURA INGALLS WILDER
(1867-1957)

*This is the world
of the short cut,
the evasive answer,
the cut corner.
Integrity has to hold
on by its fingertips
to survive.*

PAM BROWN, B.1928

SUCCESS HAS
NOTHING TO DO WITH
WHAT YOU GAIN IN LIFE
OR ACCOMPLISH FOR
YOURSELF. IT'S WHAT
YOU DO FOR OTHERS.

DANNY THOMAS

Seek out that particular
mental attitude which makes
you feel most deeply
and vitally alive, along
with which comes
the inner voice which says,
"This is the real me,"
and when you have
found that attitude,
follow it.

WILLIAM JAMES (1842-1910)

You may never know what results come from your action. But if you do nothing, there will be no result.

MAHATMA GANDHI
(1869-1948)

It is the greatest
of all mistakes to do
nothing because you
can only do little.

SYDNEY SMITH
(1771-1845)

Idealists... foolish enough to throw caution to the winds...have advanced mankind and have enriched the world.

EMMA GOLDMAN (1869-1940)

Trust people,
and they will be
true to you; treat
them greatly, and
they will show
themselves great.

RALPH WALDO EMERSON
(1803-1882)

The only real satisfaction
there is, is to be growing
up inwardly all the time,
becoming more just, true,
generous, simple, manly,
womanly, kind, active.
And this we can all do,
by doing each day
the day's work as well
as we can.

JAMES FREEMAN CLARKE
(1810-1888)

*There is no road
to success but through
a clear strong purpose.
Nothing can take its place.
A purpose is the eternal
condition of success.*

THEODORE MUNGER

*The whole thing is about
earning your own way
and you don't really get there
until you earn it.
That's the real truth.*

TINA TURNER, B.1939

I am not bound to win
but I am bound to be true.
I am not bound to succeed
but I am bound to live up
to what light I have.

ABRAHAM LINCOLN
(1809-1865)

The hallmark of courage
in our age of conformity is
the capacity to stand on one's
convictions – not obstinately
or defiantly (these are
gestures of defensiveness,
not courage)... but simply
because these are what
one believes.

ROLLO MAY

I believe that work is love in action. It is my feeling that if more people thought about their work and their lives in this way, they could accomplish so much and make great strides toward fulfilling their potential.

JEANE PINCKERT DIXON,
(1918-1997)

Kindness in words creates confidence, kindness in thinking creates profoundness, kindness in giving creates love.

LAO-TZU
(6TH CENTURY B.C.)

No act of kindness, no matter how small, is ever wasted.

AESOP, c.550 B.C.

I believe that all of us have the capacity for one adventure inside us, but great adventure is facing responsibility day after day.

WILLIAM GORDON

Do what you believe in and believe in what you do. All else is a waste of energy and time.

NISARGADATTA

Deeds, not words.

MOTTO OF
THE MCRARIE FAMILY

*Nothing on Earth
is more gladdening than
knowing we must roll up
our sleeves and move back
the boundaries of the
humanly possible once more.*

ANNIE DILLARD

A reputation
for good judgment,
for fair dealing,
for truth, and
for rectitude,
is itself a fortune.

HENRY WARD BEECHER
(1813-1887)

He has achieved
success who has lived
well, laughed often
and loved much;
who has enjoyed
the admiration and love
of good people;
who has filled his niche
and accomplished
his task; who has left
the world better than
he found it....

BESSIE A. STANLEY

Integrity
rings
like fine glass.
True, clear
and
reassuring.

PAM BROWN, B.1928

*A*chievement
doesn't come
from what we do,
but from who we are.
Our worldly power
results from our
personal power.

MARIANNE WILLIAMSON

If you think
you're too small
to have an
impact, try going
to bed with
a mosquito.

ANITA RODDICK
(1942-2007)

THE TEST OF COURAGE COMES WHEN WE ARE IN THE MINORITY.

RALPH W. SOCKMAN
(1889-1970)

Many people
do not allow their
principles to take root,
but pull them up
every now and then,
as children
do the flowers
they have planted,
to see if they are growing.

HENRY
WADSWORTH LONGFELLOW
(1807-1882)

*I*t seems to me we can
never give up longing
and wishing while we
are thoroughly alive.
There are certain
things we feel to be
beautiful and good,
and we must hunger
after them.

GEORGE ELIOT
(MARY ANN EVANS) (1819-1880),
FROM
"THE MILL ON THE FLOSS"

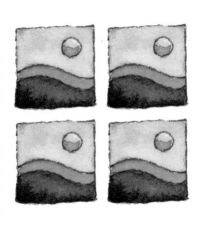

Success is
to be measured not
so much by
the position one has
reached in life,
as by the obstacles
which we have
overcome while
trying to succeed.

BOOKER T. WASHINGTON
(1856-1915)

*J*ust be what
you are
and speak from
your guts
and heart – it's all
a person has.

HUBERT H. HUMPHREY
(1911-1978)

You should always
keep your word.
All the setbacks in life
come only because you
don't keep your word....

SIVANANDA

Corruption is like
a ball of snow,
when once set a rolling
it must increase.

C.C. COLTON (1780-1832)

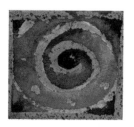

*The successful
are the people who
have fallen flat a dozen
times – but have got
to their feet again.*

PAM BROWN, B.1928

Whatever course you decide upon, there is always someone to tell you that you are wrong. There are always difficulties arising which tempt you

to believe that
your critics are right.
To map out a course
of action and
follow it to an end
requires courage.

RALPH WALDO EMERSON
(1803-1882)

Truth is like
sugar cane: even if
you chew it
for a long time, it is
still sweet.

MALAGASY PROVERB

*All the great things
are simple, and many can be
expressed in a single word:
freedom; justice; honour; duty;
mercy; hope.*

SIR WINSTON CHURCHILL
(1874-1965)

I'd rather have roses
on my table than
diamonds on my neck.

EMMA GOLDMAN
(1869-1940)

Guard within
yourself that
treasure, kindness.
Know how to give
without hesitation,

how to lose without regret, how to acquire without meanness.

GEORGE SAND (AMANDINE AURORE LUCIE DUPIN)

THE LOVE WE GIVE AWAY IS THE ONLY LOVE WE KEEP.

ELBERT HUBBARD (1856-1915)

*Gentleness is
a divine trait: nothing
is so strong as gentleness
and nothing so gentle
as real strength.*

RALPH W. SOCKMAN (1889-1970)

ONLY A LIFE
LIVED FOR OTHERS
IS WORTH LIVING.

ALBERT EINSTEIN
(1879-1955)

My feeling
is that there
is nothing in life
but refraining
from hurting
others, and
comforting those
that are sad.

OLIVE SCHREINER
(1855-1920)

We can do no great things — only small things with great love.

MOTHER TERESA (1910-1997)

If you have not often felt the joy of doing a kind act, you have neglected much, and most of all yourself.

A. NEILEN

Progress results only from the fact that there are some men and women who refuse to believe that what they know to be right cannot be done.

RUSSELL DAVENPORT

The best place to succeed is where you are with what you have.

CHARLES M. SCHWAB

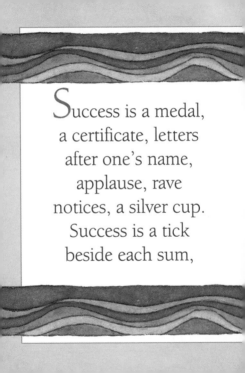

Success is a medal,
a certificate, letters
after one's name,
applause, rave
notices, a silver cup.
Success is a tick
beside each sum,

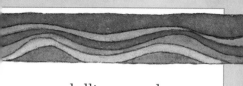

a lollipop at the
finishing line, a bright
blue ribbon
on one's swimsuit.
And success is a hug,
a kiss, a smile.

PAMELA DUGDALE

*I*t's not what you do
once in a while,
It's what you do
day in and day out
That makes
the difference.

JENNY CRAIG

The uncle who can
tell stories, sing songs,
invent games, may be
a nothing in the eyes of
the world – but he is
a crowned king in
the eyes of the children.

PAM BROWN, B.1928

To endure is
greater than to dare;
to tire out hostile fortune;
to be daunted by no
difficulty; to keep heart
when all have lost it –
who can say this is
not greatness?

WILLIAM MAKEPEACE THACKERAY
(1811-1863)

IF YOU PROPOSE
TO SPEAK, ALWAYS
ASK YOURSELF —
IS IT TRUE,
IS IT NECESSARY,
IS IT KIND?....

GAUTAMA BUDDHA
(c. 563-483 B.C.)

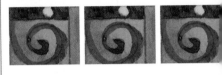

The ideals which
have lighted my way,
and time after time
have given me new
courage to face
life cheerfully, have
been kindness,
beauty, and truth....

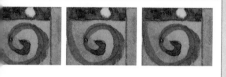

The trite subjects
of human efforts –
possessions, outward
success, luxury –
have always seemed
to me contemptible.

ALBERT EINSTEIN
(1879-1955)

Personal success,
business success,
built upon
materialism alone,
are empty shells
concealing...
saddened lives.

GEORGE R. WHITE

If success depends
upon misusing
those about you
– opt for failure!

PAM BROWN, B.1928

*L*ife presents
a never ending series
of opportunities
to perform little acts
of caring. Don't miss
even one. They are
our opportunities
to become great.

STUART AND LINDA
MACFARLANE

Kind words
can be short
and easy to speak,
but their echoes
are truly endless.

MOTHER TERESA
(1910-1997)

*O*ne does what
one must – in spite
of personal
consequences,
in spite of obstacles
and dangers and
pressures – and that
is the basis
of all morality.

SENATOR
JOHN F. KENNEDY
(1917-1963)

You don't get
to choose how you're
going to die.
Or when. You can
only decide how you're
going to live. Now.

JOAN BAEZ, B.1941

If we are facing
in the right
direction,
all we have to do
is to keep on
walking.

ANCIENT BUDDHIST
EXPRESSION

Make no little
plans; they have
no magic....
Make big
plans, aim high in
hope and work.

DANIEL H. BURNHAM

Far away there in the sunshine are my highest aspirations. I may not reach them but I can look up and see their beauty, believe in them and try to follow them.

LOUISA MAY ALCOTT (1832-1888)

Do continue to believe
that with your feeling
and your work you are
taking part in the
greatest; the more strongly
you cultivate in yourself
this belief, the more will
reality and the world go
forward from it.

RAINER MARIA RILKE
(1875-1926)

*Whatever games are played
with us, we must play no games
with ourselves, but deal
in our privacy with the last
honesty and truth.*

RALPH WALDO EMERSON
(1803-1882)

The right way is not always
the popular and easy way.
Standing for right when
it is unpopular is a true test
of moral character.

MARGARET CHASE SMITH

*T*o be a good
human being is to have
a kind of openness
to the world,
an ability
to trust uncertain
things beyond
your control.

MARTHA NUSSBAUM

It is easy in the world
to live after the world's
opinion; it is easy in
solitude to live after our own;
but the great person is the
one who in the midst of
the crowd keeps with
perfect sweetness the
independence of solitude.

RALPH WALDO EMERSON (1803-1882)

The voice of conscience is so delicate that it is easy to stifle it; but it is also so clear that it is impossible to mistake it.

MME. DE STAËL (1766-1817)

You gain strength, courage, and confidence by every experience in which you really stop to look fear in the face. You are able to say to yourself, "I lived through this horror. I can take the next thing that comes along."

ELEANOR ROOSEVELT
(1884-1962)

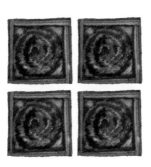

ONE PERSON WITH
A BELIEF IS EQUAL
TO A FORCE OF
NINETY-NINE WHO
ONLY HAVE INTERESTS.

JOHN STUART MILL
(1806-1873)

*T*ruth and love
are two of the most
powerful things in
the world; and when
they both go together
they cannot easily
be withstood....

RALPH CUDWORTH

Much sheer
effort goes into
avoiding truth:
left to itself,
it sweeps in like
the tide.

FAY WELDON,
FROM
"THE RULES OF LIFE"

If you see good
in people, you radiate
a harmonious loving
energy which uplifts
those who are around
you. If you can
maintain this habit,
this energy will turn
into a steady flow
of love.

ANNAMALAI SWAMI

BE BIG ENOUGH

TO SERVE

OTHER PEOPLE.

CLAUDE PEPPER
(1900-1989)

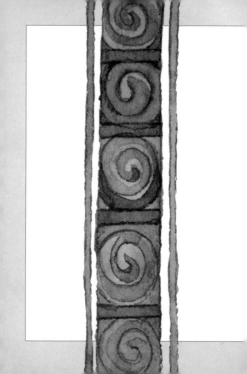

Real joy comes
not from ease
or riches
or from praise,
but from
doing something
worthwhile.

SIR WILFRED GRENFELL
(1865-1940)

*A*bove all, let us
never forget that
an act of goodness
is in itself an act
of happiness. It is
the flower of a long

*inner life of joy and
contentment;
it tells of peaceful hours
and days on the
sunniest heights
of our soul.*

COUNT MAURICE
MAETERLINCK (1862-1949)

Nothing liberates
our greatness like
the desire to help,
the desire to serve.

MARIANNE WILLIAMSON

The best and most
beautiful things in the world
cannot be seen or even
touched. They must be felt
with the heart.

HELEN KELLER (1880-1968)

It had long since come
to my attention that
people of accomplishment
rarely sat back and let things
happen to them.
They went out and
happened to things.

ELINOR SMITH

The real secret of success
is enthusiasm. Yes, more
than enthusiasm, I would
say excitement. I like to see
people get excited. When
they get excited they make
a success of their lives.

WALTER CHRYSLER

*Don't let your special
character and values,
the secret that you know
and no one else does,
the truth – don't let
that get swallowed up
by the great chewing
complacency.*

MERYL STREEP, B.1949

In CHOOSING
SUCCESS —
THERE IS
THE POSSIBILITY
YOU MAY LOSE
EVERYTHING ELSE
OF VALUE.

PAM BROWN, B.1928

*The world
is a wheel always
turning.
Those who are high
go down low,
and those who've
been low go
up higher.*

ANZIA YEZIERSKA

None of us suddenly
becomes something
overnight.
The preparations have
been in the making
for a lifetime.

GAIL GODWIN, B.1937

SUCCESS
IS CARVED SLOWLY
AND
WITH CARE.

PAM BROWN, B.1928

True morality consists not in following the beaten track, but in finding out the true path for ourselves and fearlessly following it.

MAHATMA GANDHI (1869-1948)

Remember all courage is not in fighting, constancy in a good cause being the chief....

CHARLES I (1600-1649)

In the pursuit of
happiness half
the world is on
the wrong scent.
They think it
consists in having
and getting,
and in being served
by others.

Happiness is
really found in
giving and in
serving others.

HENRY DRUMMOND
(1851-1897)

*A look of sympathy,
of encouragement;
a hand reached out
in kindness.
All else is secondary.*

MAYA V. PATEL, B.1928

*W*ork hard,
play often and live
in love.

STUART AND LINDA
MACFARLANE

You have reached
the pinnacle of success
as soon as you
become uninterested
in money, compliments,
or publicity.

THOMAS WOLFE
(1900-1938)

TO HAVE GROWN WISE
AND KIND
IS REAL SUCCESS.

AUTHOR UNKNOWN

Treat people as if they were what they ought to be and you will help them become what they are capable of becoming.

JOHANN WOLFGANG
VON GOETHE (1749-1832)

Spiritual empowerment is evidenced in our lives by our willingness to tell ourselves the truth, to listen to the truth when it's

told to us, and to
dispense truth as
lovingly as possible,
when we feel
compelled to
talk from the heart.

CHRISTINA BALDWIN,
FROM
"LIFE'S COMPANION"

*T*hose who make fame
and the opinion of others
their life's goal are
always panting after it
like a thirsty dog.
They never find peace....

MARTIN GREY

A person who floats
with the current,
who does not guide themself
according to higher
principles, who has no ideal,
no convictions –
such a person is...
a thing moved, instead of
a living and moving being
– an echo, not a voice....

HENRI FRÉDÉRIC AMIEL
(1821-1881)

When we have the courage
to speak out —
to break our silence —
we inspire the rest
of the "moderates"
in our communities
to speak up and to vote
their views.

SHARON SCHUSTER

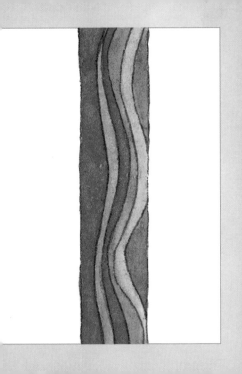

*C*ivilization is founded
on integrity of mind and
heart and action.

PAM BROWN, B.1928

*A*ll the beautiful
sentiments in the world
weigh less than a single
lovely action.

JAMES RUSSELL LOWELL
(1819-1891)

I have met brave women who are exploring the outer edge of human possibility, with no history to guide them,

and with a
courage to make
themselves
vulnerable that
I find moving
beyond words.

GLORIA STEINEM, B.1934

*Success is not
a place at which
one arrives
but rather
the spirit with
which one
undertakes and
continues
the journey.*

ALEX NOBLE

THERE ARE
NO SHORTCUTS TO
ANY PLACE
WORTH GOING.

BEVERLEY SILLS (1929-2007)

*In the war between
falsehood and truth,
falsehood wins
the first battle and truth
the last.*

MUJIBUR RAHMAN

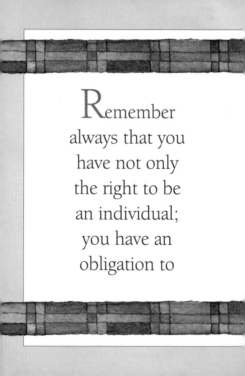

Remember
always that you
have not only
the right to be
an individual;
you have an
obligation to

be one. You cannot
make any useful
contribution
in life unless you
do this.

ELEANOR ROOSEVELT
(1884-1962), FROM
"YOU LEARN BY LIVING"

*D*o not follow
where the path
may lead.
Go, instead, where
there is no path
and leave a trail.

AUTHOR UNKNOWN

I am only one,
But still I am one.
I cannot do everything,
But still I can do
something; And
because I cannot do
everything I will not
refuse to do
the something that
I can do.

EDWARD E. HALE (1822-1909)

The thing always happens that you really believe in; and the belief in a thing makes it happen. And I think nothing will happen until you thoroughly and deeply believe in it.

FRANK LLOYD WRIGHT
(1867-1959)

WHENEVER YOU
SEE A SUCCESSFUL
BUSINESS, SOMEONE
ONCE MADE A
COURAGEOUS DECISION.

PETER DRUCKER

What after all has
maintained the human
race on this old globe,
despite all the calamities
of nature and all the tragic
failings of mankind,
if not the faith in new
possibilities and the
courage to advocate them?

JANE ADAMS

To do anything
in this world
worth doing,
we must not stand
back shivering
and thinking of

the cold and
danger, but jump
in and scramble
through as well
as we can.

SYDNEY SMITH (1771-1845)

Doubts
ARE MORE CRUEL
THAN THE
WORST OF TRUTHS.

MOLIERE (1622-1673),
FROM "LE MISANTHROPE"

That quiet
mutual gaze of
a trusting husband
and wife is like
the first moment
of rest or refuge
from a great
weariness or
a great danger.

GEORGE ELIOT
(MARY ANN EVANS)
(1819-1880)

"Henry Rackmeyer,
you tell us what
is important."
"A shaft of
sunlight at the
end of a dark
afternoon, a note
in music, and the
way the back
of a baby's neck

*smells...." "Correct,"
said Stuart.
"Those are the
important things."*

E.B. WHITE (1899-1985)

Kindnesses are like
summer flowers slipped
between the pages of
a book – their messages of
affection springing to life
again in a few years.

PAM BROWN, B.1928

If someone listens,
or stretches out a hand,
or whispers a kind word
of encouragement, or
attempts to understand
a lonely person,
extraordinary things
begin to happen.

LORETTA GIRZARTIS

To fill the hour –
that is happiness;
to fill the hour,
and leave no crevice
for a repentance
or an approval.

RALPH WALDO EMERSON
(1803-1882)

Wealth, notoriety,
place and power
are no measure of
success whatever....

WILLIAM DANFORTH

SUCCESS
IS A PROCESS,
A QUALITY OF MIND
AND WAY OF BEING,
AN OUTGOING
AFFIRMATION
OF LIFE.

ALEX NOBLE

I know the price of
success: dedication, hard work
and an unremitting devotion
to the things
you want to see happen.

FRANK LLOYD WRIGHT
(1867-1959)

The height of your
accomplishments
will equal the depth of
your convictions.

WILLIAM F. SCOLAVINO

I believe that we are solely responsible for our choices, and we have to accept the consequences of every deed, word, and thought throughout our lifetime.

ELISABETH
KUBLER-ROSS (1926-2004)

Do all the good you can,
By all the means you can,
In all the ways you can,
In all the places
you can, At all the times
you can,
To all the people you can,
As long
as ever you can.

JOHN WESLEY (1703-1791)

WHAT DO WE LIVE FOR, IF IT IS NOT TO MAKE LIFE LESS DIFFICULT FOR EACH OTHER?

GEORGE ELIOT
(MARY ANN EVANS)
(1819-1880)

You have not lived
a perfect day,
even though you have
earned your money,
unless you have done
something for someone
who will
never be able to
repay you.

RUTH SMELTZER

I long to accomplish a great
and noble task,
but it is my chief duty
to accomplish
small tasks as if they were
great and noble.

HELEN KELLER (1880-1968)

No PLEASURE IS
COMPARABLE TO THE
STANDING UPON THE
VANTAGE-GROUND OF TRUTH.

FRANCIS BACON (1561-1626)

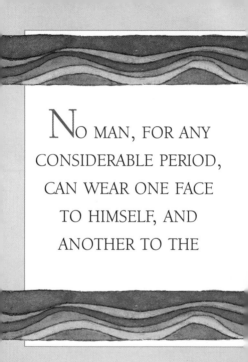

No MAN, FOR ANY
CONSIDERABLE PERIOD,
CAN WEAR ONE FACE
TO HIMSELF, AND
ANOTHER TO THE

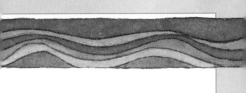

MULTITUDE, WITHOUT
FINALLY GETTING
BEWILDERED AS TO
WHICH MAY BE TRUE.

NATHANIEL HAWTHORNE
(1804-1864),
FROM "THE SCARLET LETTER"

*E*verything's a circle.
We're each responsible
for our own actions.
It will come back.

BETTY LAVERDURE, OJIBWAY

Iexpect to pass
through life but once.
If therefore, there be
any kindness I can show,
or any good thing
I can do to any fellow being,
let me do it now, and not
defer or neglect
it, as I shall not pass
this way again.

WILLIAM PENN (1644-1718)

One who knows
how to show and
to accept kindness
will be a friend
better than any
possession.

SOPHOCLES
(c. 496-406 B.C.)

If I can stop
one heart from breaking,
I shall not live in vain;
If I can ease one life
the aching, Or cool
one pain, Or help
one fainting robin
Unto his nest again,
I shall not live in vain.

EMILY DICKINSON (1830-1886)

From SUCCESS
YOU GET LOTS
OF THINGS,
BUT NOT THAT GREAT
INSIDE THING
THAT LOVE BRINGS YOU.

SAM GOLDWYN (1879-1974)

PEACE IS INEVITABLE TO THOSE WHO OFFER PEACE.

FROM
"A COURSE IN
MIRACLES"

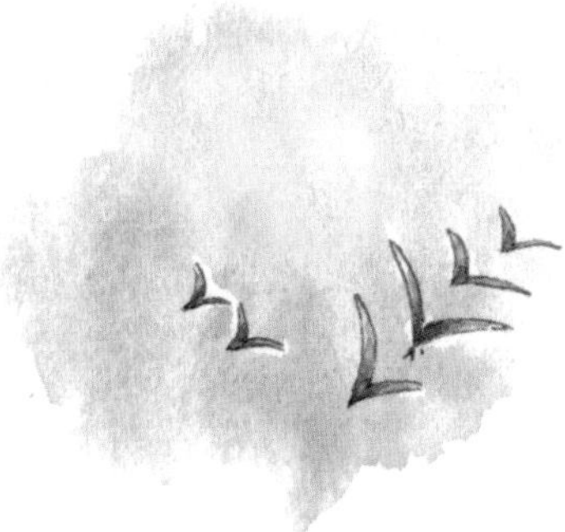

A hundred times
a day I remind
myself that my
inner and outer
life depends on
the labors of
other men, living

and dead, and
that I must
exert myself to
give in the
same measure as
I have received.

ALBERT EINSTEIN
(1879-1955)

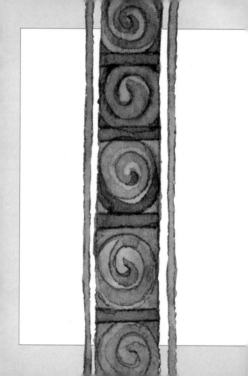

Nothing great was ever achieved without achievement. The way of life is wonderful; it is by abandonment.

RALPH WALDO EMERSON
(1803-1882)

THE CLOSER
ONE GETS TO THE TOP,
THE MORE ONE FINDS
THERE IS NO "TOP."

NANCY BARCUS

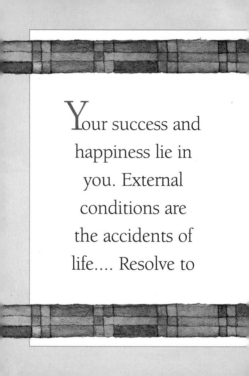

Your success and
happiness lie in
you. External
conditions are
the accidents of
life.... Resolve to

keep happy, and
your joy and you
shall form an
invincible host
against difficulty.

HELEN KELLER
(1880-1968)

Beauty is truth,
truth beauty – that is all
ye know on earth, and
all ye need to know.

JOHN KEATS (1795-1821)

TRUTH MAKES
THE FACE OF THAT
PERSON SHINE
WHO SPEAKS
AND OWNS IT....

ROBERT SOUTH (1634-1716)

To keep our faces toward change, and behave like free spirits in the presence of fate, is strength undefeatable.

HELEN KELLER
(1880-1968)

I searched
through rebellion,
drugs, diet,
mysticism, religion,
intellectualism
and much more,
only to find that
truth is basically
simple and
feels good, clear
and right.

CHICK COREA

*The secret of making
something work in your
life is, first of all,
the deep desire to make
it work: then the faith
and belief that it can work:
then to hold that clear definite
vision in your consciousness
and see it working out
step by step....*

EILEEN CADDY

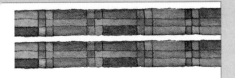

We can do anything we want to do if we stick with it long enough.

HELEN KELLER
(1880-1968)

Diamonds are only
chunks of coal,
that stuck to their jobs.

MINNIE RICHARD SMITH

I$_F$ A THOUSAND PLANS
FAIL, BE NOT DISHEARTENED.
AS LONG AS YOUR PURPOSES
ARE RIGHT,
YOU HAVE NOT FAILED.

THOMAS DAVIDSON (1840-1900)

Courage...

IS NOTHING LESS THAN
THE POWER
TO OVERCOME DANGER,
MISFORTUNE, FEAR,
INJUSTICE, WHILE
CONTINUING TO AFFIRM
INWARDLY THAT LIFE,
WITH ALL ITS SORROWS,
IS GOOD;

THAT EVERYTHING IS
MEANINGFUL, EVEN IF
IN A SENSE BEYOND
OUR UNDERSTANDING;
AND THAT THERE IS
ALWAYS TOMORROW.

DOROTHY THOMPSON

The great thing in this world is not so much where we are, but in what direction we are moving.

OLIVER WENDELL
HOLMES (1809-1894)

I began to have an idea
of my life, not as
the slow shaping of
achievement to fit
my preconceived
purposes, but as
the gradual discovery
and growth of a purpose
which I did not know.

JOANNA FIELD

*Focusing our attention –
daily and hourly –
not on what is wrong,
but on what
we love and value,
allows us to participate
in the birth of a better
future, ushered in by
the choices we make
each and every day.*

CAROL PEARSON

How one lives is,
after all, one of the rights
left to the individual –
when and if he has
opportunity to choose.

ALICE WALKER, B.1944

WE MAKE
A LIVING BY
WHAT WE GET,
BUT WE MAKE
A LIFE BY WHAT
WE GIVE.

NORMAN MACESWAN

A person's
true wealth
is the good
he or she does
in the world.

MOHAMMED

You have to count
on living every single
day in a way
you believe will make
you feel good about
your life –
so that if it were over
tomorrow,
you'd be content
with yourself.

JANE SEYMOUR, B.1951

*E*ven the smallest act of
kindness says "I care",
says "You matter", says
"I thought of you."
And so lifts the heart.

JENNY DE VRIES, B.1915

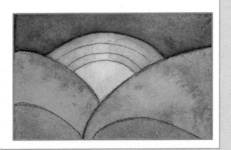

*T*here is a wonderful,
mystical law of nature
that the three things
we crave most in life —
happiness, freedom, and
peace of mind — are always
attained by giving them
to someone else.

AUTHOR UNKNOWN

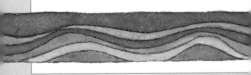

THIS IS WHAT SETS THIS
TINY OPAL OF A PLANET
OFF FROM A MILLION
GREATER WORLDS —
THE POSSIBILITY OF
KINDNESS — THE
POSSIBILITY OF CARE.

PAM BROWN, B.1928

How desperately we wish to maintain our trust in those we love! In the face of everything, we try to find reasons to trust. Because losing faith is worse than falling out of love.

SONIA JOHNSON

IT DOES NOT REQUIRE MANY WORDS TO SPEAK THE TRUTH.

CHIEF JOSEPH
(1840-1904), NEZ PERCE

At the end
of life one's
successes cease to
matter much.
Only friendships
count.

PAM BROWN, B.1928

THE LANGUAGE OF TRUTH IS UNADORNED AND SIMPLE....

MARCELLINUS AMMIANUS
(c.330-390)

Within us should always be that peace which is forever listening and open-minded.

ROMANO GUARDINI

Never, if possible, lie
down at night
without being able
to say: "I have made
one human being
at least a little wiser,
or a little happier,
or a little better
this day."

CHARLES KINGSLEY
(1819-1875)

The most solid
comfort one can fall
back upon is the thought
that the business of
one's life is to help in some
small way to reduce the sum
of ignorance, degradation
and misery on the face
of this beautiful earth.

GEORGE ELIOT
(MARY ANN EVANS)
(1819-1880)

Do noble things, do not dream them all day long.

CHARLES KINGSLEY
(1819-1875)

You can have
anything you want
if you want it
desperately enough.
You must want
it with an exuberance
that erupts through
the skin and joins
the energy that
created the world.

SHEILAH GRAHAM

W E HAVE ENOUGH
PEOPLE WHO TELL IT LIKE
IT IS — NOW WE COULD
USE A FEW WHO TELL IT
LIKE IT CAN BE.

ROBERT ORBEN, B.1927

When you look
back on your life
and count your blessings
these will not be reckoned
in terms of money
accumulated or rank
achieved. Instead what
will prove to be most
important are the deeds
you have done for others.

STUART AND LINDA MACFARLANE

Duty does not
have to be dull.
Love can
make it beautiful
and fill it
with life.

AUTHOR UNKNOWN

This is what you shall do:
love earth and sun
and animals, despise riches,
give alms to anyone that
asks, stand up for the
stupid and crazy, devote
your income and labor
to others, hate tyrants....

WALT WHITMAN
(1819-1892)

Things get better
when enough people
decide that they should
get better. Things change
when ordinary people
come together
in a common purpose.

KOFI ANNAN

*F*ollow what you love!...
Don't deign to ask
what "they" are looking for
out there. Ask what
you have inside. Follow not
your interests,
which change, but what
you are and what you love,
which will and should
not change.

GEORGIE ANNE GEYER

THIS ABOVE ALL: TO THINE OWN SELF BE TRUE.

WILLIAM SHAKESPEARE
(1564-1616),
FROM "HAMLET"

Living in balance and purity is the highest good for you and the earth.

DEEPAK CHOPRA, B.1947

The Great Spirit placed me here... to take good care of the ground and to do each other no harm.

YOUNG CHIEF

If, at the end,
all that can be said
of you is that you
were kind –
it is enough.

PETER GRAY, B.1928

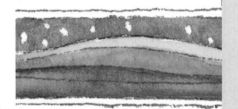

No pleasure philosophy,
no sensuality, no place
nor power, no material
success can for a moment
give such inner satisfaction
as the sense of living for
good purpose.

MINOT SIMONS

Don't

Compromise Yourself. You're All You've Got.

JANIS JOPLIN
(1943-1970)

I WANT TO BE ALL THAT I AM CAPABLE OF BECOMING....

KATHERINE MANSFIELD
(1888-1923)

*O*ne's lifework,
I have learned, grows
with the working
and the living.
Do it as if your life
depended on it,
and first thing you
know, you'll have
made a life out of it.
A good life, too.

THERESA HELBURN

Go confidently
IN THE DIRECTION OF YOUR
DREAMS! LIVE THE LIFE
YOU'VE IMAGINED.

HENRY DAVID THOREAU
(1817-1862)

If I have been of service, if I have glimpsed more of the nature and essence of ultimate good, if I am inspired to reach wider horizons of thought and action, if I am at peace with myself, it has been a successful day.

ALEX NOBLE

*T*o have a purpose
that is worthwhile,
and that is
steadily being
accomplished,
that is one of the
secrets of a life
that is
worth living.

HERBERT CASSON

WHAT IS A HELEN EXLEY GIFTBOOK?

Helen Exley Giftbooks
cover the most powerful of all
human relationships: the bonds within
families and between friends, and the
theme of personal values.
No expense is spared in making
sure that each book is as
meaningful a gift as it is possible
to create: good to give, good
to receive. You have the result in your
hands. If you have loved it –
tell others! There is no power
on earth like the word-of-mouth
recommendation of friends!

Helen Exley Giftbooks
16 Chalk Hill,
Watford, Herts
WD19 4BG, UK

www.helenexleygiftbooks.com

Illustrated by Angela Kerr.
© Helen Exley Creative Ltd 2012.

All words from Helen Exley's
collection of Values quotations.

*T*he successful
are the people who
have fallen flat a dozen
times – but have got
to their feet again.

PAM BROWN, B.1928